Captivating

Capri

FROM MARINA GRANDE TO ANACAPRI

A TRAVEL PHOTO ART BOOK

LAINE CUNNINGHAM

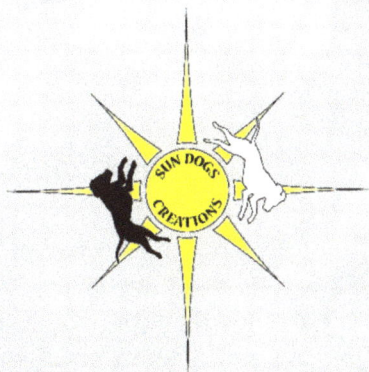

SUN DOGS CREATIONS

Captivating Capri

From Marina Grande to Anacapri

A Travel Photo Art Book

Published by Sun Dogs Creations
Changing the World One Book at a Time
Print ISBN: 9781946732996

Cover Design by Angel Leya

THE TRAVEL PHOTO ART SERIES

PRISM

ARCADIAN

HERMETIC

TAFFY

PENTHOUSE

ORCHARD

MICE & MEN

BREAKING

EXPEDITION

BRISTOL FASHION

FRENCH HARVEST

GEMSTONES

SUBMARINE

SHEEN

UPLIFT

SEA SNAKE

LOOK HOMEWARD

BLUE DREAM

TOP OF THE MORNING

TEETOTUM

SNAPLINES

PEREGRINATION

GUARDIAN

VOLCANIC

WHEELHOUSE

TRYST

TRANSITION

REST STOP

SALTIE

ROOST

PILOT WHALE

RACING

RAMBLE

GRANDEUR

About the Author

Laine Cunningham leads readers around the world. *The Family Made of Dust* is set in the Australian Outback, while *Reparation* is a novel of the American Great Plains. Her travel memoir *Woman Alone* appeals to fans of *Wild* and *Eat Pray Love*.

Novels by Laine Cunningham

The Family Made of Dust

Beloved

Reparation

Other Books by Laine Cunningham

Woman Alone: A Six-Month Journey Through the Australian Outback

On the Wallaby Track

Seven Sisters: Spiritual Messages from Aboriginal Australia

Writing While Female or Black or Gay

The Zen of Travel
The Zen of Gardening
Zen in the Stable
The Zen of Chocolate
The Zen of Dogs

Bikes of Berlin
Necropolises of New Orleans I & II
Ruins of Rome I & II
Ancients of Assisi I & II
Panoramas of Portugal
Nuances of New York
Glimpses of Germany
Impressions of Italy
Altitudes of the Alps
Knights Through the Ages
Coast of California
Utopia of the Unicorn
Flourishes of France
Portraits of Paris
Tableaus of Tbilisi
Grandeur in the Republic of Georgia
Paragons of Prague
Hidden Prague
Lidice Lives
Along the Via Appia
The Pillars of the Bohemian Paradise
Terezín and Theresienstadt

www.ingramcontent.com/pod-product-compliance
Lightning Source LLC
Chambersburg PA
CBHW051250020426
42333CB00025B/3141